Proverbs To Live By

A burden which one chooses is not felt.

ITALIAN PROVERB

Proverbs To Live By

Truths that

Live in Words

With Woodcuts

by Fritz Kredel

Selected by

Gail Peterson

HALLMARK EDITIONS

Proverbs To Live By

A book whose sale's forbidden all men rush to see, and prohibition turns one reader into three. ITALIAN PROVERB

Four things come not back—the spoken word, the sped arrow, the past life, and the neglected opportunity.

ARABIAN PROVERB

Nothing is more highly to be prized than the value of each day. GOETHE

You never know what is enough until you know what is more than enough.

WILLIAM BLAKE

If you have eaten the morsel on Wednesday, do not look for it on Thursday.

RUSSIAN PROVERB

The empty vessel makes the greatest sound.

SHAKESPEARE

Study without reflection is a waste of time; reflection without study is dangerous.

CONFUCIUS

A man too busy to take care of his health is like a mechanic too busy to take care of his tools.

SPANISH PROVERB

A lie has no legs, but scandalous wings.

JAPANESE PROVERB

Conscience gets a lot of credit that belongs to cold feet.

ANONYMOUS

As long as the sun shines one does not ask for the moon.

RUSSIAN PROVERB

Wealth is not his who has it, but his who enjoys it. FRANKLIN

The fall of a leaf is a whisper to the living.
RUSSIAN PROVERB

The grand essentials in this life are something to do, something to love, and something to hope for. ADDISON

Experience is the father of wisdom.
ANONYMOUS

Once you have missed the first buttonhole, you'll never manage to button up.
GOETHE

Perfection is attained by slow degrees; it requires the hand of time.
VOLTAIRE

A good laugh is sunshine in a house.
THACKERAY

Think not those faithful who praise all thy words and actions, but those who kindly reprove thy faults. SOCRATES

A little nonsense, now and then, is relished by the wisest men. ANONYMOUS

He who sacrifices his conscience to ambition burns a picture to obtain the ashes.

CHINESE PROVERB

From a little spark may burst a mighty flame.

DANTE

Give if thou canst, an alms; if not, afford, instead of that, a sweet and gentle word.

HERRICK

Pinch yourself and know how others feel.

JAPANESE PROVERB

Borrow trouble for yourself, if that's your nature, but don't lend it to your neighbors.

KIPLING

Think of the going-out before you enter.

ARABIAN PROVERB

Daring ideas are like chessmen moved forward; they may be beaten, but they may start a winning game. GOETHE

*The cow knows not what her tail is worth
until she has lost it.*   ANONYMOUS

The crown of a good disposition is humility.
                                    ARABIAN PROVERB

Do not choose for anyone what you do not
choose for yourself.   PERSIAN PROVERB

Asking costs little.   ITALIAN PROVERB

There is no fire like passion, there is no shark
like hatred, there is no snare like folly, there
is no torrent like greed.   BUDDHA

He fled from the rain and sat down under the waterspout.   ARABIAN PROVERB

Everyone is crazy but me and thee, and sometimes I suspect even thee.

ANONYMOUS

Where there are fish there must be water.

JAPANESE PROVERB

The wise man has long ears, big eyes and a short tongue.   RUSSIAN PROVERB

Knowledge without sense is twofold folly.

SPANISH PROVERB

He is happiest, be he king or peasant, who finds peace in his home.   GOETHE

It may come late, but it may come properly.

PERSIAN PROVERB

Forewarned, forearmed; to be prepared is half the victory.   CERVANTES

If a man could have half his wishes, he would double his troubles.   FRANKLIN

Common sense in an uncommon degree is what the world calls wisdom.   COLERIDGE

Everybody loves the tree which gives him shelter.   RUSSIAN PROVERB

He who considers too much will perform little.   SCHILLER

The sky is of the same color wherever you go.   PERSIAN PROVERB

Beat not the furnace for your foe so hot that it do singe yourself.   SHAKESPEARE

He is lifeless who is faultless.   ANONYMOUS

In proportion to the length of thy garment stretch out thy legs.   ARABIAN PROVERB

The sky is the daily bread of the eyes.   EMERSON

The greatest king must at last be put to bed with a shovel.   RUSSIAN PROVERB

What can the enemy do when the friend is cordial?   PERSIAN PROVERB

Joy and sorrow are next door neighbors.
GERMAN PROVERB

Work is often the father of pleasure.
VOLTAIRE

Love looks not with the eyes, but with the heart.   SHAKESPEARE

It is the beautiful bird which gets caged.
CHINESE PROVERB

John has one customer and Jack another.
RUSSIAN PROVERB

Talents are best nurtured in solitude; character is best formed in the stormy billows of the world.   GOETHE

The beginnings of all things are small.
CICERO

For everything you have missed you have gained something else.   EMERSON

The devil can cite Scripture for his purpose.

SHAKESPEARE

Whatever is in the heart will come up to the tongue. PERSIAN PROVERB

There's a time to wink as well as to see.

FRANKLIN

Poverty does not destroy virtue nor wealth bestow it. ANONYMOUS

13

Cleanse thy heart from greed, and thy foot shall remain free from fetters.

ARABIAN PROVERB

A man should learn to sail in all winds.

ITALIAN PROVERB

The true worth of a man is to be measured by the objects he pursues.

MARCUS AURELIUS

Make thyself a sheep, and the wolf is ready.

RUSSIAN PROVERB

How far that little candle throws his beams! So shines a good deed in a naughty world.

SHAKESPEARE

Spectators see better than actors.

PERSIAN PROVERB

To forget one's ancestors is to be a brook without a source, a tree without root.

CHINESE PROVERB

Facts do not cease to exist because they are ignored. ANONYMOUS

They wooed her and she resisted; they neglected her and she fell in love.

Good humor is one of the best articles of dress one can wear in society.

THACKERAY

All is not false that seems at first a lie.

SOUTHEY

Good words are like a string of pearls.

CHINESE PROVERB

The greatest pleasure is to do a good action by stealth and to have it found out by accident.

CHARLES LAMB

The crying cat catches nothing.

ARABIAN PROVERB

Take care that the divinity within you has a creditable charge to preside over.

MARCUS AURELIUS

The most exquisite folly is made of wisdom spun too fine.

FRANKLIN

Good manners are made up of petty sacrifices.

EMERSON

It is the peculiar quality of a fool to perceive the faults of others and to forget his own.

CICERO

The chameleon does not leave one tree until he is sure of another.

ARABIAN PROVERB

A barking dog is often more useful than a sleeping lion.

IRVING

Do not cut down the tree that gives you shade.

ARABIAN PROVERB

Exuberance is beauty.

BLAKE

Never let the bottom of your purse or your mind be seen.

ANONYMOUS

The mouse that has but one hole is soon caught.

ARABIAN PROVERB

He who knows but little, presently outs with it.

ITALIAN PROVERB

Experience is a jewel, and it had need to be so, for it is often purchased at an infinite rate.

SHAKESPEARE

All sunshine makes a desert.

ARABIAN PROVERB

Health and cheerfulness mutually beget each other.   ADDISON

Thinking is the essence of wisdom.

PERSIAN PROVERB

The soul's greatest perfection is its capacity for pleasure.   ANONYMOUS

Time ripens all things: no man is born wise.

CERVANTES

Much does he gain who learns when he loses.

ITALIAN PROVERB

Charm strikes the sight, but merit wins the soul.   POPE

Joy and Temperance and Repose slam the door on the doctor's nose.   LONGFELLOW

I had six honest serving men—they taught me all I know: Their names were Where and What and When and Why and How and Who. KIPLING

Who seeks a quarrel, finds it near at hand.
ITALIAN PROVERB

If all fools wore white caps, we should all seem a flock of geese. ANONYMOUS

The best part of beauty is that which no picture can express. BACON

The cask can only yield the wine it contains.
ITALIAN PROVERB

The soul of dispatch is decision. HAZLITT

He who sings frightens away his ills.
SPANISH PROVERB

Any plan is bad which is not susceptible to change. ITALIAN PROVERB

The remedy for injuries is not to remember them. GERMAN PROVERB

The gem cannot be polished without friction, nor man perfected without trials.

CHINESE PROVERB

The best way to get praise is to die.

ITALIAN PROVERB

He who plants trees loves others besides himself.

ANONYMOUS

He who boasts of his descent is like the potato; the best part of him is under ground.

FRENCH PROVERB

The stitch is lost unless the thread is knotted.

ITALIAN PROVERB

A man who has committed a mistake and doesn't correct it is committing another mistake.

CONFUCIUS

None are so blind as those who won't see.

ANONYMOUS

Now 'tis the spring, and weeds are shallow-rooted; suffer them now and they'll o'ergrow the garden.

SHAKESPEARE

*When your horse is on the brink of a preci-
pice it is too late to pull the reins.*

CHINESE PROVERB

Patience, and shuffle the cards.

CERVANTES

That crown is well spent which saves you
ten. ITALIAN PROVERB

It never occurs to fools that merit and good
fortune are closely united.   GOETHE

Striving to better, oft we mar what's well.
SHAKESPEARE

He has gained enough who gives up a vain
hope.   ITALIAN PROVERB

Books give not wisdom where was none before.   ANONYMOUS

No one is satisfied with his fortune, nor dis-
satisfied with his intellect.
FRENCH PROVERB

When a man is falling, every saint pushes
him.   ITALIAN PROVERB

He who falls in love with himself will have
no rivals.   ANONYMOUS

Valor lies just half-way between rashness
and cowardice.   CERVANTES

There is no one luckier than he who thinks
himself so.   GERMAN PROVERB

The riches that are in the heart cannot be stolen. RUSSIAN PROVERB

Proverbs bear age and he who would do well may view himself in them as in a looking glass. ITALIAN PROVERB

The tongue of woman is her sword, which never rusts. JAPANESE PROVERB

Make the most of yourself, for that is all there is to you. EMERSON

Keep company with good men, and you'll increase their number. ITALIAN PROVERB

When you are an anvil, be patient; when a hammer, strike. ARABIAN PROVERB

Patience is a virtue, virtue is a grace; both put together make a very pretty face. ANONYMOUS

He who is an ass and takes himself to be a stag finds his mistake when he comes to leap the ditch. ITALIAN PROVERB

A man there was and they called him mad;
the more he gave the more he had.

BUNYAN

If young men had wit and old men strength
everything might be well done.

ITALIAN PROVERB

There is nothing either good or bad but
thinking makes it so.   SHAKESPEARE

Love knows hidden paths.

ANONYMOUS

He who would have no trouble in this world
must not be born in it.

ITALIAN PROVERB

Everything has its beauty but not everyone
sees it.   CONFUCIUS

People themselves alter so much that there is
something new to be observed in them for-
ever.   AUSTEN

Fool me once, shame on you; fool me twice,
shame on me.   CHINESE PROVERB

A man shows his character by what he laughs at. GERMAN PROVERB

The business of life is to go forwards.

JOHNSON

No bird soars too high if he soars with his own wings. BLAKE

A man's teeth often bite his own tongue.

JAPANESE PROVERB

Adversity is the diamond dust Heaven polishes its jewels with.

AUTHOR UNKNOWN

He who sows discord will reap regret.

ARABIAN PROVERB

When the ship has sunk everyone knows how she might have been saved.

ITALIAN PROVERB

Time is painted with a lock before, and bald behind, signifying thereby that we must take time by the forelock, for when it is once passed there is no recalling it. SWIFT

First catch your hare, then cook it.

ANONYMOUS

A man's being in a good or bad humor depends upon his will.

JOHNSON

He saith little that loveth much.

ITALIAN PROVERB

Let thy discontents be secrets.

FRANKLIN

The weakest among us has a gift, however seemingly trivial, which is peculiar to him and which worthily used will be a gift also to his race.

RUSKIN

The path of duty lies in what is near at hand;
and men seek for it in what is remote.

JAPANESE PROVERB

Wisdom thoroughly learned will never be
forgotten. PYTHAGORAS

Those who do not feel pain seldom think
that it is felt. JOHNSON

He who is only wise lives a sad life.

VOLTAIRE

He who sees a need and waits to be asked for
help is as unkind as if he had refused it.

DANTE

The world is governed more by appearances
than by realities, so that it is fully as neces-
sary to seem to know something as to know
it. DANIEL WEBSTER

He who fears death enjoys not life.

SPANISH PROVERB

One written word is worth a thousand pieces
of gold. JAPANESE PROVERB

Fear is the tax which conscience pays to guilt.

ANONYMOUS

Little strokes fell great oaks. FRANKLIN

A small-minded man looks at the sky through a reed. JAPANESE PROVERB

One must lose a minnow to catch a salmon.

FRENCH PROVERB

It is not permitted to the most equitable of men to be a judge in his own cause.

PASCAL

The pebble in the brook secretly thinks itself a precious stone. JAPANESE PROVERB

Full many a flower is born to blush unseen.

GRAY

He who reigns within himself, and rules passions, desires, and fears, is more than a king.

MILTON

Wear a smile and have friends; wear a scowl and have wrinkles. GEORGE ELIOT

A man who is his own doctor has a fool for his patient.   ANONYMOUS

A man must insult himself before others will.
                                CHINESE PROVERB

He loses all who loses the right moment.
                                SPANISH PROVERB

The fallen blossom does not return to the branch.   JAPANESE PROVERB

Wit is the salt of conversation, not the food.
                                HAZLITT

He who lies upon the ground can fall no lower.   LATIN PROVERB

Pray devoutly, but hammer stoutly.
                                ANONYMOUS

One cannot tell what passes through the heart of a man by the look on his face.
                                JAPANESE PROVERB

The best way to know God is to love many things.   VAN GOGH

What sunshine is to flowers, smiles are to
humanity.   ADDISON

Good example is half a sermon.

ANONYMOUS

The hole the crab digs takes on the shape of
its shell.   JAPANESE PROVERB

He conquers who endures.

ITALIAN PROVERB

He is well paid that is well satisfied.

SHAKESPEARE

A man's good name is as precious to him as
its skin is to a tiger.

JAPANESE PROVERB

If there is no apple one eats a little carrot.

RUSSIAN PROVERB

Natural abilities are like natural plants, that
need pruning by study.   BACON

He has a very hard heart who does not love
May.   FRENCH PROVERB

A man with a sour face should not open a shop. JAPANESE PROVERB

One pardons to the degree that one loves.
LA ROCHEFOUCAULD

When anger arises, think of the consequences.
CONFUCIUS

The past, the present and the future are really one—they are today.
HARRIET BEECHER STOWE

At the first cup man drinks wine, at the second wine drinks wine, at the third wine drinks man. JAPANESE PROVERB

There is so much good in the worst of us, and so much bad in the best of us, that it behooves all of us not to talk about the rest of us.
ROBERT LOUIS STEVENSON

Drop by drop fills the tub.
FRENCH PROVERB

Most people are as happy as they make up their minds to be. LINCOLN

He is not laughed at who laughs at himself first. ANONYMOUS

We are shaped and fashioned by what we love. GOETHE

It is part of the cure to wish to be cured.
SENECA

The creation of a thousand forests is in one acorn. EMERSON

He who prizes little things is worthy of great ones. GERMAN PROVERB

The bird that offers itself to the net is fair game to the fowler.
JAPANESE PROVERB

God often visits us, but most of the time we are not at home. FRENCH PROVERB

Break the legs of an evil custom.
ITALIAN PROVERB

A fool can no more see his own folly than he can see his ears. THACKERAY

You can't make an omelet without breaking eggs. ANONYMOUS

The heron's a saint when there are no fish about. JAPANESE PROVERB

Where interest lags, memory lags too.

GOETHE

What is bitter to endure may be sweet to remember. ANONYMOUS

People seldom improve when they have no other model but themselves to copy after.

GOLDSMITH

A soft answer turneth away wrath; but grievous words stir up anger.

OLD TESTAMENT

For every evil under the sun, there is a remedy or there is none. If there be one, try and find it; if there be none, never mind it.

ANONYMOUS

A harper is laughed at who plays always on the same string. HORACE

If you have to kill a snake, kill it once and for all. JAPANESE PROVERB

Love is the reward of love. SCHILLER

In the fields of observation, chance favors only the prepared mind. PASTEUR

If well thou hast begun, go on; it is the end
that crowns us, not the fight.

HERRICK

No man's head aches while he comforts another. ITALIAN PROVERB

A narrow mind has a broad tongue.

ARABIAN PROVERB

Better shun the bait than struggle in the
snare. DRYDEN

What one does, one becomes.

SPANISH PROVERB

Fear less, hope more; eat less, chew more;
whine less, breathe more; talk less, say more;
hate less, love more; and all good things are
yours. SWEDISH PROVERB

Virtue cannot live in solitude; neighbors are
sure to grow up around it.

CHINESE PROVERB

The greatest difficulties lie where we are not
looking for them. GOETHE

Dost thou love life? Then do not squander time, for that is the stuff life is made of.

FRANKLIN

Daylight will peep through a very small hole.

JAPANESE PROVERB

Give the apple to the beautiful and the rose to the wise.

RUSSIAN PROVERB

Action is the proper fruit of knowledge.

THOMAS FULLER

There is a point at which even justice does injury.

SOPHOCLES

An idle brain is the devil's workshop.

ENGLISH PROVERB

Kindness is the sunshine in which virtue grows.

ANONYMOUS

Talk does not cook rice.

CHINESE PROVERB

Rich gifts wax poor when givers prove unkind.

SHAKESPEARE

Following happiness is like chasing the wind, or clutching the shadow.

JAPANESE PROVERB

He who sows his land trusts in God.

SPANISH PROVERB

We have two ears and one mouth that we may listen the more and talk the less.

GREEK PROVERB

Flowers are God's thoughts of beauty taking form to gladden mortal gaze.

ANONYMOUS

They who know the truth are not equal to those who love it, and they who love it are not equal to those who find pleasure in it.

CHINESE PROVERB

If you wish another to keep your secret, first keep it yourself.

LATIN PROVERB

Do not think it wasted time to submit yourself to any influence that will bring upon you any noble feeling. RUSKIN

Having a good wife and rich cabbage soup, seek not other things.

RUSSIAN PROVERB

Never esteem anything as of advantage to thee that shall make thee break thy word or lose thy self-respect.

MARCUS AURELIUS

A man of words and not of deeds is like a garden full of weeds. ANONYMOUS

The morning steals upon the night, melting the darkness. SHAKESPEARE

One is wiser in the morning than in the evening. RUSSIAN PROVERB

Anger is as a stone cast into a wasp's nest.

INDIAN PROVERB

If you walk on snow you cannot hide your footprints. CHINESE PROVERB

Let your hook be always cast; in the pool where you least expect it, there will be a fish.

OVID

He that wrestles with us strengthens our nerves and sharpens our skill.

EDMUND BURKE

Good nature, like a bee, collects honey from every herb. Ill nature, like the spider, sucks poison from the sweetest flower.

ANONYMOUS

Compare your griefs with other men's and they will seem less. SPANISH PROVERB

When the ear will not listen, the heart escapes sorrow. CHINESE PROVERB

Most powerful is he who has himself in his own power. SENECA

A word of kindness is better than a fat pie.
RUSSIAN PROVERB

One dog yelping at nothing will set ten thousand straining at their collars.
JAPANESE PROVERB

Arrogance diminishes wisdom.
ARABIAN PROVERB

When we cannot find contentment in ourselves, it is useless to seek it elsewhere.
LA ROCHEFOUCAULD

For a marriage to be peaceful the husband should be deaf and the wife blind.
SPANISH PROVERB

Words are like leaves; and where they most abound, much fruit of sense beneath is rarely found. POPE

When the fox cannot reach the grapes he says they are not ripe. GREEK PROVERB

We cannot all be masters.

SHAKESPEARE

Do not remove a fly from your friend's head with a hatchet. CHINESE PROVERB

That is an empty purse that is full of other men's money. ANONYMOUS

When the fruit is scarcest its taste is sweetest. IRISH PROVERB

Have patience and the mulberry leaf will become silk. SPANISH PROVERB

The daughter of a crab does not give birth to a bird. CHINESE PROVERB

It is in men as in soils, where sometimes there is a vein of gold which the owner knows not of. SWIFT

It's no use going to the goat's house to look for wool. IRISH PROVERB

Three things too much and three too little are pernicious to man: to speak much, and know little; to spend much, and have little; to presume much, and be worth little. CERVANTES

The more a man knows, the more he forgives. ANONYMOUS

You cannot sew buttons on your neighbor's mouth. RUSSIAN PROVERB

Don't see all you see, and don't hear all you hear. IRISH PROVERB

Every cloud engenders not a storm.

SHAKESPEARE

'Tis not the dying for a faith that's so hard; 'tis the living up to it that is difficult.

THACKERAY

Men carry their superiority inside, animals outside. RUSSIAN PROVERB

One pound of learning requires ten pounds of common sense to apply it.

PERSIAN PROVERB

Hide not your talents, for use they were made; what's a sun-dial in the shade?

FRANKLIN

Vegetables of one's own raising are not relished—those from other's gardens are the best. CHINESE PROVERB

One can see the heavens through a needle's eye. JAPANESE PROVERB

A small hole can sink a big ship.
RUSSIAN PROVERB

Whatever necessity lays upon thee, endure; whatever she commands, do. GOETHE

Better be alone than in bad company.
ANONYMOUS

The web of our life is of a mingled yarn, good and ill together. SHAKESPEARE

A cynic is a man who knows the price of everything and the value of nothing.
OSCAR WILDE

He who allows his day to pass by without practicing generosity and enjoying life's pleasures is like a blacksmith's bellows—he breathes but does not live.
SANSKRIT PROVERB

A foolish consistency is the hobgoblin of little minds. EMERSON

Measure thy cloth ten times, thou canst cut it but once. RUSSIAN PROVERB

Though patience be a tired mare, yet she will plod. SHAKESPEARE

Go home and make a net if you desire to get fishes. CHINESE PROVERB

A long life may not be good enough, but a good life is long enough. ANONYMOUS

Long sleep makes a bare back.
IRISH PROVERB

If you wish your merit to be known, acknowledge that of other people.
ORIENTAL PROVERB

Time is too slow for those who wait, too swift for those who fear, too long for those who grieve, too short for those who rejoice; but for those who love, time is eternity.
HENRY VAN DYKE

The journey of a thousand miles starts with a single step. CHINESE PROVERB

Our bodies are our gardens, to which our wills are gardeners. SHAKESPEARE

He who plants thorns must never expect to gather roses. ARABIAN PROVERB

They who give have all things; they who withhold have nothing.

HINDU PROVERB

The man who makes the first bad move always loses the game.

JAPANESE PROVERB

Wit without discretion is a sword in the hand of a fool. SPANISH PROVERB

Words are the voice of the heart.

CONFUCIUS

If you go to war pray once; if you go on a sea journey pray twice; but pray three times when you are going to be married.

RUSSIAN PROVERB

To live in hearts we leave behind is not to die. ANONYMOUS

Wisdom is ofttimes nearer when we stoop
than when we soar.   WORDSWORTH

You cannot hang everything on one nail.
                                      RUSSIAN PROVERB

A vacant mind is open to all suggestions as a
hollow building echoes all sounds.
                                      CHINESE PROVERB

We walk by faith, not by sight.
                                      NEW TESTAMENT

A guest has not to thank the host, but the
host the guest.   RUSSIAN PROVERB

If love be timid it is not true.
                                      SPANISH PROVERB

It takes little effort to watch a man carry a
load.   CHINESE PROVERB

The greater the obstacle the more glory in
overcoming it.   MOLIERE

If you wish another to keep your secret, first
keep it yourself.   LATIN PROVERB

A star, however willing, cannot help the moon. CHINESE PROVERB

All things are less dreadful than they seem. ANONYMOUS

Many take by the bushel and give by the spoon. GERMAN PROVERB

No one knows what he can do till he tries. LATIN PROVERB

What the young one begs for, the grown-up throws away. RUSSIAN PROVERB

Courage and perseverance have a magical talisman, before which difficulties disappear and obstacles vanish into air. JOHN QUINCY ADAMS

Men are men; the best sometimes forget. SHAKESPEARE

A little and a little, collected together, become a great deal; the heap in the barn consists of single grains, and drop and drop make the inundation. SAADI

Much wealth will not come if a little does not go. CHINESE PROVERB

Well done is better than well said.

FRANKLIN

It is not enough to be busy; so are the ants. The question is: What are we busy about?

THOREAU

The proper study of mankind is man. POPE

The future belongs to him who knows how to wait. RUSSIAN PROVERB

The beautiful is as useful as the useful.

VICTOR HUGO

It is only when the cold season comes that we know the pine and cypress to be evergreens.

CHINESE PROVERB

Tyrant custom makes a slave of reason.

ANONYMOUS

The same fire purifies gold and consumes straw. ITALIAN PROVERB

You look for the horse you ride on.

RUSSIAN PROVERB

Beggars mounted run their horse to death.

SHAKESPEARE

Love the truth but pardon error.

VOLTAIRE

Kindness is the golden chain by which society is bound together.

GOETHE

One's good deeds are only known at home; one's bad deeds far away.

CHINESE PROVERB

Each goodly thing is hardest to begin.

SPENSER

That day is lost on which one has not laughed. FRENCH PROVERB

A man wrapped up in himself makes a very small package. ANONYMOUS

He who handles pitch besmears himself.

GERMAN PROVERB

Hurry is only good for catching flies.

RUSSIAN PROVERB

Quiet minds cannot be perplexed or frightened but go on in fortune or misfortune at their own private pace, like a clock during a thunderstorm.

ROBERT LOUIS STEVENSON

He who is good for making excuses is seldom good for anything else. FRANKLIN

In the kingdom of the blind men, the one-eyed is king.   ANONYMOUS

A needle is sharp only at one end.
                           CHINESE PROVERB

Uncertainty and expectation are the joys of life.   CONGREVE

Justice is the insurance we have on our lives, and obedience is the premium we pay for it.
                           WILLIAM PENN

Love is a canvas furnished by Nature and embroidered by imagination.
                           VOLTAIRE

Life is a mirror: if you frown at it, it frowns back; if you smile, it returns the greeting.
                           THACKERAY

He jests at scars that never felt a wound.
                           SHAKESPEARE

The chameleon, who is said to feed upon nothing but air, has of all animals the nimblest tongue.   SWIFT

The apples on the other side of the wall are the sweetest. ANONYMOUS

Look for a thing till you find it and you'll not lose your labor. CHINESE PROVERB

One can advise comfortably from a safe port.
SCHILLER

Everywhere in life the true question is, not what we have gained, but what we do.

CARLYLE

When one door shuts another opens.
SPANISH PROVERB

Do not despise an insignificant enemy or a slight wound. GERMAN PROVERB

An eel held by the tail is not yet caught.
ANONYMOUS

Love your enemies, for they tell you your faults. FRANKLIN

A good book is the precious life-blood of a master spirit. MILTON

He who rides a tiger is afraid to dismount.

CHINESE PROVERB

Shun idleness. It is a rust that attaches itself to the most brilliant of metals.

VOLTAIRE

A man often pays dear for a small frugality.

EMERSON

Thatch your roof before rainy weather; dig your well before you become parched with thirst.

CHINESE PROVERB

He that will not apply new remedies must expect new evils. BACON

The longest day will have an end.

ANONYMOUS

A mile walked with a friend has only one hundred steps. RUSSIAN PROVERB

While we consider when to begin, it becomes too late. LATIN PROVERB

Brevity is the soul of wit.

SHAKESPEARE

He who brings himself into needless dangers dies the devil's martyr. ANONYMOUS

Though honey is sweet, do not lick it off a briar. IRISH PROVERB

Rotten wood cannot be carved.

CHINESE PROVERB

Conceit is to nature what paint is to beauty; it is not only needless, but it impairs what it would improve. POPE

Not the cry, but the flight of the wild duck,
leads the flock to fly and follow.

CHINESE PROVERB

Mellow nuts have the hardest rind.

ANONYMOUS

Help thy brother's boat across, and lo! thine
own has reached the shore.

HINDU PROVERB

The dress does not make the friar.

SPANISH PROVERB

Make every bargain clear and plain, that
none may afterwards complain.

ANONYMOUS

To sow is less difficult than to reap.

GOETHE

Friendship improves happiness, and abates
misery, by doubling our joy, and dividing our
grief.   ADDISON

If the child does not cry, the mother knows
not its wants.   RUSSIAN PROVERB

Truth will rise above falsehood as oil above
water. CERVANTES

Give every man thine ear, but few thy voice.
SHAKESPEARE

The only way to compel men to speak good
of us is to do it. VOLTAIRE

Desire beautifies what is ugly.
SPANISH PROVERB

He who has health, has hope; and he who
has hope, has everything.
ARABIAN PROVERB

When it rains, it rains on all alike.
ANONYMOUS

Good temper, like a sunny day, sheds a ray
of brightness over everything: it is the sweet-
ener of toil and the soother of disquietude!
WASHINGTON IRVING

A man's faults all conform to his type of
mind. Observe his faults and you may know
his virtues. CONFUCIUS

Good, better, best; never rest till good be better, and better, best. ANONYMOUS

Burdens become light when cheerfully borne. OVID

He who peeps in at his neighbor's window may chance to lose his eyes. ARABIAN PROVERB

Confidence is a plant of slow growth. NEW TESTAMENT

Only those who have the patience to do simple things perfectly will acquire the skill to do difficult things easily. SCHILLER

An empty sack cannot stand up. RUSSIAN PROVERB

It is with narrow-souled people as with narrow-necked bottles; the less they have in it, the more noise they make in pouring it out. POPE

"Luck" is a very good word if you put a "P" before it. ANONYMOUS

If you tickle yourself, you can laugh when
you like. RUSSIAN PROVERB

Conceit is God's gift to little men.

ANONYMOUS

Eavesdroppers never hear any good of themselves. FRENCH PROVERB

Little and often fills the purse.

GERMAN PROVERB

Who will eat the kernel of the nut must break
the shell. ANONYMOUS

Our senses don't deceive us: our judgment
does. GOETHE

Silence betokens consent.

PERSIAN PROVERB

A diamond with a flaw is preferable to a
common stone with none.

CHINESE PROVERB

Fools need advice most, but wise men only
are the better for it. FRANKLIN

The reward of a thing well done, is to have done it. EMERSON

One cannot learn to swim in a field.
SPANISH PROVERB

All work is as seed sown; it grows and spreads, and sows itself anew.
ANONYMOUS

It is not only what we do, but also what we do not do, for which we are accountable.
MOLIERE

Winter comes fast on the lazy.
IRISH PROVERB

Manners are the happy ways of doing things; each one a stroke of genius or of love, now repeated and hardened into usage.
EMERSON

Habits are first cobwebs, then cables.
ANONYMOUS

Patience is the key of joy; but haste is the key to sorrow. ARABIAN PROVERB

When the cat mourns for the mouse do not take her seriously.   JAPANESE PROVERB

A man's foibles are what makes him lovable.

GOETHE

Tact is the unsaid part of what you think; its opposite, the unthought part which you say.   HENRY VAN DYKE

The seeking for one thing will find another.

IRISH PROVERB

Those who know when they have enough are rich.   CHINESE PROVERB

Fritz Kredel, who created the colored woodcuts for Proverbs To Live By, is a world-celebrated book illustrator with a special gift for capturing the picturesque spirit of a text. His many books include Fairy Tales of the Brothers Grimm, Edward Lear's A Book of Ballads, and the famous folio Soldiers of the American Army. Many of his works are now collectors' items. He lives in New York.

Set at The Castle Press in Trump Mediäval, a Venetian face designed by Professor Georg Trump, in Munich. Printed on Hallmark Eggshell Book Paper. Designed by Harald Peter.